WHO AM I?

Identity in Christ

Jerry Bridges

To Don, whose gracious perseverance in the face of
adversity has been a constant challenge to me.
– Jerry Bridges

CruciformPress

© 2012 by Jerry Bridges. All rights reserved.
CruciformPress.com | info@CruciformPress.com

"Jerry Bridges' gift for simple but deep spiritual communication is fully displayed in this warm-hearted, biblical spelling out of the Christian's true identity in Christ."

J. I. Packer, Theological Editor, *ESV Study Bible;* author, *Knowing God, A Quest for Godliness, Concise Theology*, and more; retired Professor of Theology, Regent College

"I know of no one better prepared than Jerry Bridges to write *Who Am I?* He is a man who knows who he is in Christ and he helps us to see succinctly and clearly who we are to be. Thank you for another gift to the Church of your wisdom and insight in this book."

R.C. Sproul, founder, chairman, president, Ligonier Ministries; executive editor, *Tabletalk* magazine; general editor, *The Reformation Study Bible*; author, *The Holiness of God* and more than seventy other books

"*Who Am I?* answers one of the most pressing questions of our time in clear gospel categories straight from the Bible. This little book is a great resource to ground new believers and remind all of us of what God has made us through faith in Jesus. Thank the Lord for Jerry Bridges, who continues to provide the warm, clear, and biblically balanced teaching that has made him so beloved to this generation of Christians."

Richard D. Phillips, senior minister, Second Presbyterian Church, Greenville, SC; chairman, Philadelphia Conference on Reformed Theology; vice chairman, Alliance of Confessing Evangelicals; author of *Jesus the Evangelist, The Masculine Mandate,* and many more

Table of Contents

CruciformPress

Clear, inspiring, gospel-centered
CruciformPress.com

We publish clear, useful, theologically sound, and helpful books for Christians and other curious people. Books that make sense and are easy to read, even as they tackle serious subjects.

We do this because the good news of Jesus Christ—the gospel—is the only thing that actually explains why this world is so wonderful and so awful all at the same time. Even better, the gospel applies to every single area of life, and offers real answers that aren't available from any other source.

These are books you can enjoy, benefit from, and remember. Check us out and see.

Who Am I? - Identity in Christ

Print ISBN:	978-1-936760-47-3
ePub ISBN:	978-1-936760-49-7
Mobipocket ISBN:	978-1-936760-48-0

INTRODUCTION

Who are you?

- The man sitting to my left at a dinner referred to himself as a carpenter. Carpentry is his vocation, but it is not who he is.
- A lady with a broken marriage said to a friend, "I am just a failure." Although she had failed in her marriage, that is not who she is.
- I grew up in moderate poverty. To this day, my default answer to the question, "Who am I?" is, "I am the little boy growing up on the dirt street alongside the railroad track." But that is not who I am.

These three responses illustrate the common tendency to answer the question "Who am I?" in terms of some subjective experience. Many of us answer in terms of our vocation. Others focus on a particularly formative or emotional experience.

I serve with the Navigators collegiate ministry, primarily focusing on staff development. But I am familiar enough with the student scene to know that many young people arrive at college from difficult family backgrounds, or carrying the baggage of their own sinful lifestyles during their high school days. As a result, many of them have low or even negative self-images. Many, if honest, would answer the question "Who am I?" in terms of their negative or sinful experiences.

As Christians, however, our identity is to be found in our relationship with Christ, not in our subjective and often negative life experiences. In our ministry to students, therefore, we seek to help them become aware of their "position and identity in Christ," so that their answer to the question "Who am I?" is based on what it means to be "in Christ."

There is no short and simple answer to the question, "Who am I in Christ?" That position involves both privileges and responsibilities. It involves some tremendously astounding truths about us, but also faces us with some sobering facts that are just as true.

In this book we are going to look at eight different answers to the question, "Who am I?" It is my prayer that these eight answers will give us a balanced, biblical view of what it means to be in Christ.

One
I AM A CREATURE

When we begin to answer the question "Who am I?" we need to start with the most basic truth about us: we are created beings. "So God created man in his own image, in the image of God he created him; male and female he created them" (Genesis 1:27). While being made in God's image puts us on an entirely different plane from any of the animals, we are still creatures. This makes us both dependent upon God and accountable to God.

Utterly Dependent

One of the most basic truths about all creatures is that we are dependent on God. Psalms 145:15-16 says, "The eyes of all look to you, and you give them their food in due season. You open your hand; you satisfy the desire of every living thing." This passage refers primarily to the animal kingdom, but the principle of dependency applies to human beings as well.

Food. In most respects, we share our dependencies with the animal kingdom. However, there is at least one significant difference. God ordained that we humans should work to produce much of our food (see Genesis 2:15), and in this very work we can develop a sense of independence from God. We begin to think that our material needs are met solely through our own hard work or (the modern-day equivalent) our business acumen, which provides us with the means to purchase food. God specifically warned the nation of Israel of this danger when he said,

> Beware lest you say in your heart, "My power and the might of my hand have gotten me this wealth." You shall remember the LORD your God, for it is he who gives you power to get wealth, that he may confirm his covenant that he swore to your fathers, as it is this day. (Deuteronomy 8:17-18)

Life and breath. We have a need more basic than food; we are dependent on God for our very life, even our breath. Acts 17:25 says, "nor is he served by human hands, as though he needed anything, since he himself gives to all mankind life and breath and everything." Every breath we breathe is a gift from God. And every day of life is also a gift from him. As David said, "My times are in your hands" (Psalms 31:15).

Plans. We are dependent on God for the execution of our plans. Everyone makes plans. In fact, life would be rather chaotic without plans. And we assume that we will usually carry out those plans. But James said this is not so. Rather he says,

> Come now, you who say, "Today or tomorrow we will go into such and such a town and spend a year

there and trade and make a profit" — yet you do not know what tomorrow will bring. What is your life? For you are a mist that appears for a little time and then vanishes. Instead you ought to say, "If the Lord wills, we will live and do this or that." (James 4:13-15)

James does not rebuke his readers for making plans, even plans to make a profit in business. What he condemns is presumptuous planning—the attitude that we can carry out our plans apart from the sovereign will of God.

In the summer of 2011, I was scheduled to teach at a collegiate summer training program in Branson, Missouri. Plans were made and tickets were purchased. My wife had even arranged to have dinner with a cousin living nearby. But instead of being in Branson that week, I spent several days in a local hospital due to an unexpected heart problem. My experience is not unusual. Most of us can recall instances when some big plans we had made were overruled by God's plan for us. Truly we are dependent on God to carry out every detail of our lives, whether it is a major vacation or a trip to the corner grocery store.

Abilities. We are dependent upon God for our abilities, our spiritual gifts, and our talents. The apostle Paul says in 1 Corinthians 4:7, "What do you have that you did not receive? If then you received it, why do you boast as if you did not receive it?"

Every so often I encounter one of those "self-made men," the kind who might claim to have "pulled himself up by his own bootstraps." He likes to tell you how he started from nothing and became successful. Some of you reading this book may have experienced that. But why did God bless your plans, why did God bless your efforts? What do you have that you did not receive? Every ability—mental ability or business ability, whether it's in the fine arts or athletics or whatever it might be—it's all a gift from God. We are utterly dependent upon him.

Obviously, the wider culture in which we live today fails to recognize that we are dependent on God for everything. Often, it rejects the idea outright. And as the influence of the culture almost inevitably infiltrates our thinking as Christians, we can begin to forget we are totally dependent on God for every aspect of our lives.

To elaborate on our dependence before God just a bit more, we can see our dependence as falling into two general categories: physical fragility and spiritual vulnerability.

Physically Fragile

As dependent creatures, we are physically fragile—subject to accidents and diseases and all kinds of things. My first wife, who is now enjoying the presence of God, was always in good health. She seldom had a cold and never had the flu. The only time she had to be in a hospital was to deliver babies. But one day she went to the doctor for what she thought would be a routine examination. Before the day was over we knew she had cancer, and 17 months later she died. We are physically fragile. Regardless of how healthy we may appear today we do not know what tomorrow will bring for us.

A friend who was a missionary in Africa died at the early age of 62. Doctors did an autopsy to determine the cause of this untimely and rather sudden death and discovered that he was a victim of a combination of germs and viruses and parasites that he had picked up during years of service in Africa. Another friend was riding his bicycle early one morning for exercise and accidentally drove into a curb and went right over the handlebars, hitting his head on the concrete and breaking just about every bone in his face. We are very fragile.

Proverbs 27:1 says we do not know what a day will bring. For that matter we don't even know what the next hour will bring. You can undoubtedly supply your own stories of friends or relatives who have experienced unexpected illnesses or life-shattering accidents. So we need to recognize how fragile we really are, and as a result become aware of our total dependence on God.

Spiritually Vulnerable

As dependent creatures we are also spiritually vulnerable. We have three enemies: the world, the devil and our own sinful flesh. The world—the totality of humanity that is set in opposition to God—is constantly seeking to conform us to its own standards and values. The devil comes to us disguising himself as an angel of light (2 Corinthians 11:14), seeking to sow doubt in our minds as to the love and faithfulness of God toward us. And then, worst of all, we have our sinful flesh which constantly strives against the Spirit who resides in us.

In the field of espionage there is often a person called

a *mole*. Typically, a mole works inside a sensitive area of government, blending in as an apparent "team player," when in fact he or she is serving as the eyes and ears of an opposing power. This person is actually a traitor, to all appearances working for one government, but in actuality working for its enemy.

In many ways, our sinful flesh acts as a mole. It is constantly responding to the allurements of the world and the enticements of the devil, and is constantly seeking to collaborate with them. And so we are very vulnerable spiritually.

The recognition that we are physically fragile and spiritually vulnerable should make us more conscious of our complete dependence on God. As I write these words I have just passed my eighty-second birthday. As I get older it seems that God is increasing my own awareness of my dependence on him in every area of life. Do-it-your-self projects around the house that used to come easily to me don't anymore. So I often find myself crying out to God to help me complete ordinary tasks that I used to do routinely. I think this growing sense of dependency is due to more than growing older. I think it is part of God's process of maturing me as a believer. The same thing is true in both my physical life and my spiritual life. The truth, however, is that in my younger years I was just as dependent on God as I am now. I just did not recognize it.

Morally Accountable

Human beings are also different from other creatures in that God created us in his image. Central among all the things that may be included in that truth is the fact that we possess a moral dimension; we have the ability to know right from wrong, and the ability to obey or disobey God. This means that as moral creatures we are accountable to God. God stressed this accountability to the first man, Adam. Genesis 2:16-17 says, "And the LORD God commanded the man, saying, 'You may surely eat of every tree of the garden, but of the tree of the knowledge of good and evil you shall not eat, for in the day that you eat of it you shall surely die.'" With that commandment, God makes Adam accountable.

This theme of accountability continues throughout the Bible. In Genesis 4, God holds Cain accountable for the murder of his brother. In Exodus 20, God gives Israel the Ten Commandments, obviously implying accountability for obedience. In Psalms 119:4 we read, "You have commanded your precepts to be kept diligently." Jesus said, "If you love me you will keep my commandments" (John 14:15). Paul said, "So then each of us will give an account of himself to God" (Romans 14:12). Finally, at the end of the age, the dead will be judged according to what they had done (Revelation 20:13). So from the creation of Adam until the end of time God holds human beings accountable to him for keeping his commandments. We are not free simply to disobey God and expect it will make no difference. This is what it means to be morally accountable.

But just as we tend to ignore or even reject the reality of our total dependence on God, so we frequently ignore or reject our accountability to him. Some years ago I began to read a book titled *The Day America Told the Truth*. It was so discouraging I didn't finish it. The book was written by two men who had traveled throughout the United States, randomly interviewing people about their private lives and moral standards. They concluded that each person in America has, in effect, developed his own ten commandments. That is, as a nation we no longer see ourselves as accountable to God, only to self.

This is the attitude of the world we live in. And if we do not proactively remind ourselves that we are accountable to God, we can begin to think the same way—as long as we stay away from flagrant sins such as murder and sexual immorality, we tend to think that simply following our own code of conduct is good enough.

When I was a schoolboy, we had to memorize the poem *Invictus*, by William Ernest Henley. To this day I recall the lines, "I am the master of my fate; I am the captain of my soul." At the time, we thought of that poem as teaching courage and fortitude. But it is actually a defiant statement of independence from God. And to some degree the sentiment behind those words is the default attitude of every human being. We don't like to be dependent and accountable, yet we are. Those words accurately apply to us as creatures, made in the image of God.

Application

What application should we make of the truth that we are dependent, fragile, vulnerable, and accountable?

Humility. First, this realization should produce

humility. Recognizing that I am absolutely dependent on God for every breath and every morsel of food; seeing that I am accountable to God for every thought, every word, and every action; and realizing how often I fail to honor God in these ways — these should produce a deep and abiding sense of humility.

Gratitude. Second, it should produce profound gratitude. Everything good in me or around me, whether spiritual or material, is a gift from God. More importantly, as one who has trusted in Christ as my Savior, I know that he has taken on himself the accountability for all my sins and has fully paid the penalty for my every act of disobedience.

I am a creature, created in the image of God, fully dependent on him and fully accountable to him.

Two
I AM IN CHRIST

We have begun to answer the question "Who am I?" with the fact that we are all creatures, created in the image of God, dependent on him, and accountable to him. This is true of everyone born into the world whether we realize it or not. But for those of us who have trusted in Christ as our Savior, there is much more to our identity than simply being creatures.

The answer to the question, "Who am I as a Christian?", is far more elaborate and wonderful than the answer to the simpler (if still profound) question, "Who am I as a human being?" Once we are converted, there are seven additional glorious truths that come into play as essential components of our identity. These will constitute our focus for the remainder of this book.

As we seek to answer that more elaborate question, it is beyond dispute that we must start with the fact that we are "in" Christ Jesus.

What does it mean to be in Christ? Is it a question of location, like being in a house? Is it something like belonging to a club or an organization? No, the term "in Christ" is the apostle Paul's shorthand expression for being united to Christ. It is one of Paul's favorite expressions, and (including similar expressions such as "in him" or "in the Lord") Paul uses it more than 160 times in his letters. Clearly this is an important concept in Paul's theology. And it should be an important concept for us because *all the remaining answers to the question "Who am I?" are based upon the fact that we are in Christ, or we are united to Christ.*

This of course begs the question, what does it mean to be united to Christ? To answer it, we begin with 1 Corinthians 15:22, "For as in Adam all die, so also in Christ shall all be made alive." Note the two expressions "in Adam" and "in Christ." And again in 1 Corinthians 15:45, Paul refers to "the first man Adam" and to "the last Adam," who is clearly Christ. What Paul is getting at in these two verses is that in God's way of dealing with humanity there are only two men, Adam and Christ. *All the rest of us are represented before God by one or the other of these two men.*

Adam as Our Representative

In verse 22 Paul said, "in Adam all die." This idea is developed more completely in Romans 5:12-19. Verse 12 says, "Therefore, just as sin came into the world through one man, and death through sin, and so death spread to all men because all sinned...." This verse is a reference to Adam's sin of eating the forbidden fruit as recounted in Genesis 3. God had said, "but of the tree of the knowledge of good and evil you shall not eat, for in the day that you eat of it you shall surely die." Adam, along with Eve, ate, and they both died. They instantly died spiritually, and they would eventually die physically. But Adam was not an ordinary man so that the consequences of his sin would fall only on him.

Rather, Adam had been appointed by God to represent the entire human race. As a result, the consequences of his sin fell upon all humanity. When Paul writes in verse 12, "and so death spread to all men because all sinned…," he is referring, not to our own individual sins, but to the fact that we were so united to Adam as our representative head that when he sinned we all sinned, and so we all suffered the consequences of Adam's sin.

This idea of the representative nature of Adam's sin is further developed in verse 18, "Therefore, as one trespass led to condemnation for all men," and again in verse 19, "For as by the one man's disobedience the many were made sinners." Note especially in verse 19 the expression, "many were made sinners." All humanity (with the exception of Christ, who was not descended from Adam) suffered the consequences of Adam's sin. We were *made* sinners. As each of us comes into the world, we come as sinners by nature.

In answer to the question "Who am I?" we would therefore have to say, "I am a sinner." That is why David acknowledged, "Surely I was sinful at birth, sinful from the time my mother conceived me" (Psalms 51:5 NIV). David said the nature he received at conception was a sinful nature. Why was this true? It was because David, like you and me, was represented by Adam in the garden, and through the disobedience of Adam, David was made a sinner.

Picture two men, Adam and Christ, standing before God. Behind Adam stands all of humanity representatively united to him. We all come into this world "in Adam." Because of that, Paul's descriptive words in Ephesians 2:1-3 are true of every one of us before we trust Christ. Here is what he wrote:

> And you were dead in the trespasses and sins in which you once walked, following the course of this world, following the prince of the power of the air, the spirit that is now at work in the sons of disobedience-- among whom we all once lived in the passions of our flesh, carrying out the desires of the body and the mind, and were by nature children of wrath, like the rest of mankind.

Paul's description of our dismal condition can be summed up in three expressions:

- Spiritually dead
- Slaves (to the world, the devil, and our sinful passions)
- Objects of God's wrath

Think of that! As one "in Adam" you came into the world an object of God's wrath. It doesn't matter whether we were born of Christian parents or pagan parents. We are all born "in Adam" and so an object of God's wrath. All because Adam sinned.

Not only all of humanity, but creation itself suffered the consequences of Adam's sin. Though in Genesis

3:17-19, God refers specifically to cursing the ground, Paul in Romans 8:19-22, speaks of the futility of all creation. So we all come into the world spiritually dead, objects of God's wrath, and into a natural environment that is under the curse of God. That is what it means to be "in Adam."

Christ as Our Representative

The other man standing before God is the "last Adam," namely the Lord Jesus Christ. Just as God appointed Adam to represent all of humanity, so he appointed Christ to represent all who trust in him as Savior. We have looked at the consequences of Adam's representative act in Romans 5:18-19. Now observe the contrasting effects of Christ's work on behalf of all who trust in him. Verse 18: "so one act of righteousness leads to justification and life for all men." And in verse 19, "so by the one man's obedience the many will be made righteous."

For the sake of clarity, we need to draw out Paul's artful use of language in verses 18 and 19.

- Verse 18: "as one trespass led to condemnation for all men, so one act of righteousness leads to justification and life for all men." In this verse, the first appearance of "all men" refers to our universal condemnation. The second appearance refers to the universal offer of salvation, not the universal existence of salvation. There is universal condemnation, and there is a universal way of escape, yet not all will escape.

- Verse 19: "For as by the one man's disobedience the many were made sinners, so by the one man's obedience the many will be made righteous." Here, Paul follows the same artful use of language as in verse 18. The first appearance of "the many" is a universal statement, while the second appearance refers exclusively to those who come to Christ.

In each verse, therefore, the first "all" and "many" refer to the fact that all humanity has suffered the consequences of Adam's sin. The second "all" and "many" refer only to all those who trust in Christ and are "in him."

What are the results of being in him? We will explore these in detail in subsequent chapters, but for now I want to call our attention to the principle by which God operates.

Obedience and Disobedience

In Deuteronomy 28, Moses sets before the nation of Israel two alternatives: obedience and disobedience. The results of obedience are tremendous blessings. The results of disobedience are horrible curses. These particular blessings and curses are all temporal in nature and refer specifically to the nation of Israel in the Promised Land. But at the same time they are an expression of the eternal principle by which God operates: blessings for obedience and curses for disobedience.

By his perfectly obedient life over thirty-three years, Christ earned the blessings of God. By his death on the cross he experienced the curse for disobedience. As our representative, all that he did in both his life and death accrues to our benefit. Someone has said it like this: "He lived the life we could not live, and died the death we deserved to die." Or again, "He was treated as we deserved to be treated in order that we might be treated as he deserved to be treated."

When we think of the work of Christ, we usually think of his death to pay for our sin. We call this his "substitutionary atonement," in that he died in our place, as our substitute, to satisfy the justice of God for our sins. But what is it that makes this substitution valid? How could God's justice be satisfied when a perfectly innocent man suffers punishment on behalf of those who actually deserve it?

The answer is that Christ stood before God as our representative. He assumed the responsibility for our obedience to the law of God, *and* he assumed the responsibility to render to God satisfaction for our disobedience. All this because we are "in him," that is, we are united to him in a representative way.

The Living Union

This truth of Christ's representative union with us is foundational to all that we will be considering in subsequent chapters as we seek to answer the question, "Who am I?" But there is also a whole other dimension of our union with Christ that is equally exciting and that will help us understand who we are. That is what we call our living union with Christ.

This living union is best explained by Jesus' use of

the vine and branch metaphor in John 15:1-5. Just as the branch shares in the life and nourishment of the vine, so we as believers share in the life of Christ. This living union is affected by the Holy Spirit who lives within us (See 1 Corinthians 6:19-20), and who imparts to us the spiritual vitality of Christ himself.

As a young Christian I did not realize what it meant to be in a living union with Christ. My concept of my relationship to Christ was that he was in heaven and I was on earth. To me, prayer was like a long distance phone call to heaven, in which I might get through or I might not. My Christian life was largely one of self-effort.

One day in a time of discouragement I said to myself, "How can someone in Christ be as discouraged as I am?" At the time I had no idea of what it meant to be in Christ. To me it was just another expression for being a Christian. But as soon as I said those words, the thought came into my mind, (planted, I think, by the Holy Spirit), *What did you just say? What does it mean to be in Christ?*

So I went to my favorite place to spend time alone with God and began to ponder the question, "What does it mean to be in Christ?" I had memorized various verses which had in them the words "in Christ," or "in him" or "in the Lord," but as I said, the words had no special meaning for me. But that day, as those verses began to flow through my mind, I saw the truth in John 15:1-5 that I had a vital living relationship with Christ. I was actually a partaker of his life. I didn't need to make long-distance calls to heaven. No, I was in him, and through his Spirit he was in me.

Of all the Scriptures that went through my mind that morning, the most exciting to me was 1 Corinthians 1:30 which in the King James Version says, "But of him are ye in Christ Jesus, who of God is made unto us wisdom, and righteousness, and sanctification, and redemption." The thought that was so exciting to me was that it is *of God* that I am in Christ Jesus. I didn't, as it were, get into Christ of my own doing. It was God who united me to him. It was by his action that I am in Christ Jesus.

Isn't that encouraging? God is the one who unites us to Christ. To use Paul's expression, he is the one who has placed us in Christ. That means we can never get out. We didn't do anything to get in, and we can't do anything to get out. It's all of God.

Even today, fifty-five years later, that verse brings sparkle to my life. I often wake up discouraged about something. But as I get dressed and walk down the hall to the kitchen to make a cup of coffee, 1 Corinthians 1:30 will come to my mind and I say to myself, "God, it is of you that I am in Christ." And all of a sudden I will break into a great big smile, and the discouragement is gone.

The idea that our being in Christ is all of God, and further, because we are in Christ, his very life flows into us, could lead to the impression that we have no responsibility or part to play in this relationship. First of all, although it is indeed of God that we are united to Christ, we are united to him *by faith*. But where do we get the faith? It is the gift of God (See Ephesians 2:8-9 and Acts 16:14). But though this faith is given to us, we must still exercise it.

Having exercised faith to believe in Christ, we must

also exercise faith to draw upon the life and nourishment that comes to us from Christ through our living union with him. There are some who teach that just as the branch does nothing to receive the nourishment of the vine, so we do nothing to receive the life and energy of Christ. But this presses the analogy too far. Just as Christ is not entirely like a vine, we are not entirely like branches. Human beings are unique in that we have been created in the image of God. He has, among other things, given us minds to think with and wills which we may exercise, and he works through our minds and wills; not apart from them.

So in summary, we see that there are two related but distinct aspects of being in Christ, that is, united to him.

Representative union. The first is the representative union by which Jesus assumed all our responsibility to perfectly obey the law of God, and also assumed our penalty of death for not obeying. We will explore the results of this in the next two chapters.

Living union. The second aspect is the living union through the Holy Spirit, by which we, by faith, draw upon the nourishment and power of the living Christ to enable us to live the Christian life.

Further development of these two aspects will help us to answer the question, "Who am I?"

By the work of God, I am no longer in Adam:
I am in Christ, through a union that is both living and
representative.

Three
I AM JUSTIFIED

To be "in Christ" is the most basic identity of a Christian, so much so that all other answers to the question "Who am I?" are based on, or drawn from, that identity: this is the summation of our first two chapters. In this chapter and those that follow, we will address six implications or aspects of what it means to be "in Christ."

The most important of these is that, "I am justified." Although this statement represents the very heart of the gospel, it is not an easy concept to communicate or grasp. The idea understandably raises questions such as:

- What does it mean to be justified?
- How does one become justified?
- How can I make "I am justified" a subjective reality with respect to my own identity question?

What Does It Mean to be Justified?

To begin to answer this first question, let's look at Galatians 2:15-16.

> We ourselves are Jews by birth and not Gentile sinners; yet we know that a person is not justified by works of the law but through faith in Jesus Christ, so we also have believed in Christ Jesus, in order to be justified by faith in Christ and not by works of the law, because by works of the law no one will be justified.

In this passage, Paul says that we are justified, not by works of the law, but through faith in Jesus Christ. *Justified* is an evaluative term based on one's obedience to a law. It is a legal or courtroom evaluation. To be justified means that one has been declared "right" according to the appropriate law. In Paul's writings, especially in Romans 3 and 4, as well as Galatians 2, to be justified means to be declared righteous by God with respect to his law. It also means to be *accepted and treated by God as such*.

The great mystery and wonder of justification, and the thing we must grasp if we are to truly understand it, is how God can declare us righteous with respect to his law, when in actual fact we have disobeyed that law, and continue to disobey it on a more or less regular basis.

The Curse of the Law

In understanding how it is that God can justify sinners, we first need to see that we are not justified by works of the law — that is, by our own obedience to the law of God. Paul is emphatic about this. Note that in the one long sentence encompassed by Galatians 2:15-16, he repeats this idea three times.

Why can we not be justified or counted righteous by God through obedience to his law? The answer is found in Galatians 3:10, "For all who rely on works of the law are under a curse; for it is written, 'Cursed be everyone who does not abide by all things written in the Book of the Law, and do them.'" In this verse Paul sets an absolute standard: we can only expect to be justified by works of the law through *perfect* obedience to *all* the requirements of God's law.

Someone has counted that there are just over 600 laws given in the Old Testament, but Jesus summed them all up in two: "You shall love the Lord your God with all your heart and with all your soul and with all your mind … And the second is like it: You shall love your neighbor as yourself" (Matthew 22:37-39). Without unpacking what obedience to these two laws might look like in our lives today, suffice it to say that while Jesus did fully obey both of those commandments, no other human being has ever come close to fully obeying *either one* of them. Yet Paul says that unless we obey all things written in the book of the law, we are under a curse.

No school I know of requires an overall grade of 100 to pass a course. Usually an average of 70 is sufficient. Most people naturally assume that God "grades" in a similar fashion, and what's more, that they have probably earned a passing grade. Yet Paul says we must obey *all* things in God's law *perfectly*, and anything less places us under God's curse. So we see that all who rely on their own obedience to the law as their means of justification, instead of being counted righteous by God, are actually under his curse.

So if we seek to be justified, or counted righteous, by God, we have two options:

1. We can rely on our own righteousness.
2. We can exercise faith in Christ.

Paul calls the first option "works of the law," and guarantees us that it will result in our being cursed by God, for it is clearly impossible for us to do what God requires. But the second option does, in fact, result in our being justified. Why is this true? The best answer is found in 2 Corinthians 5:21, one of the most important verses in the Bible: "For *our* sake *he* made *him* to be sin who knew no sin, so that in him we might become the righteousness of God."

There are three "persons" mentioned in this verse, either collectively or individually.

"**He.**" This refers to God the Father—the actor of this verse.

"**Him.**" This refers to the Lord Jesus Christ—the subject of the Father's action.

"**Our.**" This term, from that opening phrase "for our sake," refers to all of us collectively. And who are we? You and I are the people described in Ephesians 2:1-3 as spiritually dead; slaves to the world, the devil, and our own sinful passions; and by nature objects of God's wrath. In Romans 5:6-10, Paul describes us as ungodly, sinners, and enemies of God. This is not a pretty picture. The "our" of 2 Corinthians 5:21 does not refer to nice people seeking to obey God but to people who are enemies of God and objects of his wrath.

The astonishing thing about this verse is that the violent actions of God the Father toward his Son were done "for our sake"—for the sake of the only guilty ones in the entire scenario. This demands further exploration. But before we see *what* God did toward his Son, let's first consider the statement that he, the Son, "knew no sin."

He Knew No Sin

Jesus did not have a sinful nature such as we have because he was not descended from Adam. You and I are slaves to our own sinful passions, but Jesus had no sinful passion. He was tempted externally by the devil (Matthew 4:4-10), and by the sinful environment in which he lived, but *there was no internal response to those temptations.* He had no sinful desires. His heart was totally united in its devotion and obedience to God. Jesus *knew no sin.*

Other New Testament writers make the same point. Hebrews 4:15 says Jesus was tempted in every respect as we are, yet without sin. 1 Peter 2:22 says he committed no sin, and 1 John 3:5 says, "in him there is no sin." So the four major writers of the New Testament letters concur: Christ was sinless; at every instant he obeyed perfectly the moral law of God. But even stronger than the testimony of these four writers are the words of Jesus himself.

In John 8, Jesus gets into an increasingly hostile dialogue with some of the Jews. They claim God as their Father, but in response to them Jesus says, "You are of your Father the devil." This contradiction of the Jews' lofty claim would have infuriated them. Then Jesus asks, "Which one of you convicts me of sin?" As Jesus spoke those words, gathered around him were not only a group of Jews who hated him and wanted nothing more than to be able to find sin in him, but also present were twelve disciples who had been with Jesus day and night, seven days a week. He could only dare to ask such a question because he knew the answer. He knew he was utterly without sin. He was absolutely and rightly confident that neither his enraged adversaries nor his closest friends could bring a single charge of sin against him.

Earlier in John 8:29, Jesus presents his self-evaluation, saying, "I always do the things that are pleasing to him [the Father]." On this point, we even have the testimony of God the Father. On two occasions—in Matthew 3:17 at Jesus' baptism, and again in Matthew 17:5 on the Mount of Transfiguration—God the Father speaks from heaven saying, "This is my beloved Son with whom I am well pleased." God could not have said those words if there had been even one occasion of sin in Jesus' life. The New Testament could not be more clear regarding the sinlessness, the perfect obedience to his Father, of the Lord Jesus Christ.

Isaiah saw God the Father sitting on his throne and heard the seraphim calling out "holy, holy, holy." The Hebrew language used triple repetition to speak of something in limitless terms. In his absolute sinlessness, his perfect obedience to God and the law of God, the Jesus who walks the pages of the New Testament is infinite in holiness in precisely the same way, and in exactly the same degree, as God the Father is infinite in holiness. Jesus in his humanity was just as holy as God sitting on his throne. Not one iota of difference.

He Was Made to Be Sin

Next, consider what God did to this absolutely sinless one, this one who lived a perfectly obedient life for 33 years. God *made him to be sin*.

This is not "made" in the sense of *created*, for God the Son has always been and always will be. Nor is this "made" in the sense of *forced*, for Jesus always obeyed the Father willingly. This is "made" in the sense of *caused*. By this rather strange expression, "made him to be sin," Paul is saying that God caused Jesus to bear the weight and guilt of our sin. In the plan and purpose of God the Father, he caused Jesus to become sin for us—again, with Jesus' cooperation, despite the unimaginable anguish and torment involved. God took all of our collective sin down through the ages, all of it, and laid it upon Christ. Every sin that we commit in thought, word, deed, and motive was heaped upon him. He was made to be sin.

Isaiah 53:6 says, "All we like sheep have gone astray; we have turned—everyone—to his own way; and the Lord has laid on him the iniquity of us all." We are all sinners. We have all gone astray, all turned to our own way, yet God has taken all of our sin and charged it to Christ. As Peter says, "He himself bore our sins in his body on the tree" (1 Peter 2:24).

Give serious thought to what the Bible is saying here. For the sake of us who are sinners, who are ungodly, who are enemies of God, the Father punished his Son. For us, God took all of our sin and heaped it upon Christ, the Lord Jesus. Consider Isaiah 53:5, "But he was wounded for our transgressions; he was crushed for our iniquities;

upon him was the chastisement that brought us peace, and with his stripes we are healed." Verse 10 says, "Yet it was the will of the LORD to crush him." It could be translated, as it was in the King James Version, that "it pleased the LORD" to do this. That is an astounding statement. It pleased God to crush his own son. Why did it please God to do this? Is God a sadist? Is God the proverbial cruel father who beats his son? No, it pleased God because God wanted to do something for us, for our sake.

Jesus did not go the cross and die involuntarily. Rather, he said, "I lay down my life that I may take it up again. No one takes it from me, but I lay it down of my own accord." (John 10:17-18). And Paul in Galatians 2:20 says, "I live by faith in the son of God, who loved me and gave himself for me." What God the Father did to Jesus, Jesus voluntarily submitted to for the sake of our salvation.

We Become the Righteousness of God

The third truth in 2 Corinthians 5:21 is "so that in him we might become the righteousness of God." God made Jesus to be sin so that we might become the righteousness of God. This raises the question, "What is this righteousness of God?" The answer to that question is found most clearly in Philippians 3:9, "and be found in him, not having a righteousness of my own that comes from the law, but that which comes through faith in Christ, the righteousness from God that depends on faith."

This righteousness has nothing to do with the striving for righteousness, through the law, that Paul rightly declares to be a futile pursuit. Rather, it is the perfect righteousness of Christ lived out over 33 years, which comes to us through faith.

Second Corinthians 5:21 is often called The Great Exchange, and it works like this. Imagine your life as a moral ledger in which every action, every thought, every word, and every motive is recorded. That's pretty grim because even our very best deeds are like a polluted garment in the eyes of God (Isaiah 64:6). But God takes your sin and removes it from your ledger and charges it to the ledger of the Lord Jesus Christ. The Savior bears the penalty for all your sin.

You then are left with a clean but empty ledger, so God does something else. He takes the perfect obedience, the perfect righteousness of Christ from his ledger and transfers it to your ledger. In computer terms you might think of this as "copy and paste," in the sense that the same righteousness, even though it has been given to you, is still available to every other Christian and everyone who will come to Christ in the future.

Now you have a ledger that no longer catalogs your sin, but instead bears only the record of 33 years of absolutely perfect righteousness. How can God do this? How can a just God completely wipe all sin off your ledger, and replace it with the perfect righteousness of Christ?

Because we are *in Christ*. He, as our representative, stands justly charged with our sin and pays its penalty through his death. And because he is our representative, God can justly credit his perfect righteousness to us. So we can say, as Paul essentially says in Galatians 2:20, that when Jesus died on the cross, we died on the cross. And when he lived a perfect life, we lived a perfect life. Because we are *in him*.

Summary. This is what it means to be justified.

1. Our sins are forgiven because they were charged to Christ.
2. The perfect righteousness of Christ has been fully credited to us.

There are two plays on the word *justified* that may help us see this more clearly. You can think of it as meaning "just as if I had never sinned." That is, it does not matter how vile and long-standing your sin is. When you trust in Christ as Savior, God looks at you just as if you'd never sinned.

To state the same thing in the opposite way, you can also think of *justified* as meaning "just as if I had always obeyed." That's the way God sees you because he sees you clothed with the perfect righteousness of Christ.

How Does One Become Justified?

Paul answers this question quite clearly and emphatically in Galatians 2:15-16 when he says, three times, that it is by faith in Jesus Christ. What is faith? We sometimes hear someone say, "I took a leap of faith." If this is a leap toward nothing in particular, a leap into emptiness, the statement is meaningless. Faith always has to have an object, and clearly for Paul, the object of faith is Jesus Christ, who through his sinless life and sin-bearing death made it possible for all who trust in him to be justified before God.

This faith is like the two sides of a coin. On one side is "renunciation." On the other side is "reliance." In order to trust in Christ we must first of all renounce any trust in our own perceived righteousness. Then we must rely completely on the finished work of Christ in both his life and death. That's how we are justified.

How Does Justification Become a Subjective Reality?

For the answer to this question, we go to Galatians 2, which begins to discuss our justification in verse 15, and continues through verse 21. At the end of verse 20, Paul says, "And the life I now live in the flesh I live by faith in the Son of God, who loved me and gave himself for me."

Paul is speaking in the present tense: "the life I *now* live." However, justification is a point-in-time event. The moment you trusted in Christ you were justified. And because justification is a point-in-time event, it is a *past* event, whether it took place five minutes ago or fifty years ago. That's why Paul can speak of justification as a past event in Romans 5:1, "Therefore, since we have been [past tense] justified by faith." But in Galatians 2:20 he speaks of it in the present tense, "the life I now [today] live in the flesh I live by faith in the Son of God."

So we see that, for Paul, justification was not only a *past event* but also a *present reality*. Every day Paul looked outside of himself, to Christ and his finished work, and saw himself righteous in the sight of God, because he was in Christ.

We all need to learn to live like Paul. Every day we too

must look outside ourselves to Christ and see ourselves justified before God because of our representative union with Christ. Most of us have "good days"—when life pretty much goes along as we desire and we have no serious struggles with sin—and "bad days"—when in one way or another we are conscious of struggling with sin all day long. It may be the sin of wicked imaginations, resentment toward someone, distrust of God, or a hundred other ways in which our flesh (sinful nature) tends to get the upper hand.

On our good days we think God must surely be pleased with us and is smiling at us. We forget, as we saw earlier, that *all our righteous deeds are like polluted garments* in the sight of God (Isaiah 64:6). On our bad days we tend to think we have lost the favor of God because of our sin. We forget that *he no longer counts our sin against us* because Jesus has already born that sin in his body on the cross.

This is not to say that we should not take our sin seriously. We do need to confess it and repent of it. But the greatest motivation for doing that is to reflect on the fact that Jesus bore those very sins you committed that day in his body on the cross, and God has forgiven you because Jesus was crushed for those sins.

So in order to experience the subjective reality of our justification we must every day look outside of ourselves to Christ. About twenty-five years ago I heard on a taped message the expression "preach the gospel to yourself every day." That is what we must learn to do if we are to enjoy the present reality of our justification. That is what

Paul did two thousand years ago when he wrote, "And the life I now live in the flesh I live by faith in the Son of God who loved me and gave himself for me" (Galatians 2:20).

I am justified, I am righteous before God, because God has charged my sin to Christ and credited to me his perfect righteousness.

Four
I AM AN ADOPTED SON OF GOD

Suppose you are a convicted serial killer sitting on death row awaiting execution, guilty of every charge for which you have been imprisoned. One day the prison warden comes to your cell door and announces that you have been fully pardoned. You are now free. But then the warden tells you that the governor who pardoned you has also adopted you. You are to go live in his home, take his family name, and become heir to his estate.

What?!?

When it comes to spiritual adoption, this is essentially what God has done for us. He has pardoned us by forgiving us of our sins. He has clothed us in the perfect righteousness of his Son. And then he adopts us into his family. In fact, Paul tells us in Ephesians 1:4-5 that this was God's plan from the beginning: he had predestined us for adoption before the foundation of the world.

As we begin to consider our status as adopted sons of God, we need to understand its meaning, and its relationship to justification.

- Justification secures our legal relationship with God as judge. In justification God declares that we are righteous in Christ.
- Adoption secures our family relationship with God. Through adoption God makes us his children.

Although we distinguish between justification and adoption, we should never separate them. They always go together in God's actions toward us. Adoption cannot occur apart from justification, and justification always results in adoption.

In one sense adoption takes our relationship with God to a higher level. Think of the serial killer and the governor. The governor can pardon the killer with a few strokes of his pen. He doesn't have to get personally involved. But to adopt the serial killer, he does have to get personally involved. By adopting him he has become personally responsible for both his welfare and his behavior.

An analogy usually breaks down at some point, and the one in the previous paragraph certainly does. The governor can pardon by a few strokes of his pen, but God cannot do that. He pardoned us at infinite cost to himself through sending his only Son to live and die in our place.

Inheritance

The primary Scripture passages on the subject of adoption are Romans 8:15-17 and—the more complete treatment—Galatians 3:25-4:7. As we look at this section of Scripture, the first thing that strikes us is Paul's use of the word *sons* instead of *children*. Paul is not being gender-specific and ignoring women. In Galatians 3:27-29 he makes it clear that both males and females are included in the category of sons. Then why the word *sons*? Because Paul was placing a priority on communicating clearly to his immediate audience.

In the Jewish culture of the day, only males were eligible to receive a part of the family inheritance. So, far from putting down women or ignoring them, he is actually making them equal with men in sharing the family inheritance. We are all one in Christ Jesus, spiritual offspring of Abraham, and equally heirs of God's promise.

Adoption in Paul's day was completely different from our practice today. In our modern culture, adoption usually refers to the adoption of an infant or small child. In the Greco-Roman culture, a childless man would adopt a mature young man to continue the family name and to receive the family inheritance. In the Jewish culture, adoption was the recognition that a son had reached an age of maturity whereby the authority and resources of the father would be passed on to him. In either case it was the family inheritance that was in view.

Paul's emphasis in his treatment on adoption is simply on the fact that we have become heirs of God. As he says in Romans 8:16-17, "and if [we are] children, then heirs—heirs of God and fellow heirs with Christ." And in Galatians 3:15 through 4:7, his main point is that being a "son" means being an heir (See 3:18, 3:29, 4:1, 4:7).

Our culture doesn't value the concept of inheritance as it did in the past, primarily because overall economic conditions have changed so much. Consider the difficulty of simple survival in the first century. The vast majority of people lived in what we would consider abject poverty, with few possessions and little or no economic cushion. The proportion of relatively wealthy people today is far, far higher than it was then. Any sort of substantial inheritance in that day was not simply a nice addition to your net worth, as it often is today. It was a completely life-changing event, a rescue from the futility of subsistence living, an elevation from one kind of life to a completely different, exceptionally rare, and far better kind.

That is what our inheritance is like as heirs. And our inheritance is not that of some unusually wealthy person, but of God himself. We have been adopted by Father God, and that fact has completely changed our future.

Granted, we have yet to fully come into our inheritance, and will not until resurrection day. This is why, following his brief treatment of adoption in Romans 8:15-17, Paul puts so much emphasis on hope.

Hope. Paul begins his brief discourse on hope (Romans 8:18-25) with the statement, "For I consider that the sufferings of this present time are not worth comparing with the glory that is to be revealed to us" (v 18). Why does he begin the subject of hope with the idea of suffering in this life? Because suffering in one form or another is the inevitable lot of most believers. And one of the many benefits of suffering is that it tends to draw us away from the allurements of this life, even the legitimate ones, and turns our attention to our eternal inheritance.

I have had about a half-dozen events or trips in my adult life that I looked forward to with great anticipation.

In each case, God has in some way blighted them with some disappointment or even trial. Why? Is God a sadist who delights to dash our expectations of a joyous time? Of course not. I don't know the mind of God, but I think it is one of his ways of drawing my heart away from even the legitimate pleasures of this life to my heavenly reward. God wants us to, as Paul says in Colossians 3:2, "Set your minds on things that are above, not on things that are on earth."

The word *hope* in our everyday vocabulary usually means no more than wishful thinking— "I hope it will not rain on our picnic today." But in the New Testament it most often means "confident expectation" in the promised eternal inheritance (See Romans 8:24, Hebrews 11:1, and 1 Peter 1:3-4). And Peter says of this inheritance that it "is imperishable, undefiled, and unfading, kept in heaven for you" (1 Peter 1:4).

I came to appreciate the meaning of Peter's words when I experienced an inheritance that proved to be perishable. Some years ago I inherited the house which my father and step-mother had bought many years before. Unfortunately, after my father died, my step-mother unwittingly allowed the house—primarily the foundation and the roof—to fall into a state of disrepair. When I engaged a realtor to sell the house, she told me that it was not saleable in its present condition. To make a long and tortuous story short, after all the expensive repairs were done, I ended up selling the house for $2000 less than I had paid for the repairs.

Paul says our inheritance will be just the opposite.

Let's go back to Paul's contrast between our sufferings and the glory of our inheritance that is to be revealed to us.

My parent's house was a modest one in a low cost-of-living area, so in 1990 the price I hoped to receive at its sale was only about $45,000. That is actually about what I paid for the extensive repairs, and then ended up taking a $2,000 loss just to sell the house. But suppose their house had been an elegant one in the high-priced area of town, and I had sold it for 4.5 million dollars. Then my repair cost would have been only one percent of the sale price, really a bargain for the return I received. Paul was basically saying that this is how we should view our eternal inheritance. The sufferings we experience in this life are not worth comparing—they are not even one percent of the glory of our inheritance. To use some hyperbole to help us grasp what Paul is saying, suppose I had sold the house, not for 4.5 million dollars, but for 45 million. Then the $45,000 I had spent on repairs would truly not be worth comparing with my return. That is the contrast Paul is drawing between our sufferings and our coming glory.

I do not mean to minimize the pain and heartache of the difficult experiences of this life. The Scripture itself says that for the moment (that is, in this life), all the disciplines of adversity seem painful rather than pleasant (Hebrews 12:11). Nor does Paul minimize our sufferings. He simply says they are not worth comparing with the glory of our inheritance that is to come. He does not minimize our pain, rather he maximizes our inheritance.

This is what it means to be adopted sons of God. To return to the illustration of the serial killer and the governor who adopts him, the just-pardoned murderer not only becomes a part of the governor's family, he also becomes heir to all of the governor's valuable estate. That pardoned criminal has a secure inheritance, and that fact alone has changed his life, but he does not yet possess or enjoy his inheritance in full. It is similar for us in that, in this life, our inheritance is always in the future, so we look forward to it with expectant hope.

I grew up in the 1930s Great Depression when many families struggled to make ends meet, and in an area where old-fashioned country gospel music was popular. Later, as an adult with a more mature outlook on Christianity, I realized that a lot of that music was rather shallow. But there was one consistent theme that ran through those songs: hope. Because life was so difficult for so many believers, they tended to look forward with hope to their eternal inheritance, and that hope was reflected in their music—hope that God would help believers "make it to the end," and then usher them into the joy and blessing of his loving presence.

Today, with our far more affluent culture, we have virtually lost sight of our eternal inheritance and the importance of hope. Yet God intends for part of our identity as those "in Christ" to be the recognition that the full realization of our identity will only come when we receive our eternal inheritance.

Abba! Father!

Paul's emphasis on our future inheritance as the most significant result of our adoption does not mean there is no benefit in this present life of being an heir. Far from it. In both Romans 8:15 and Galatians 4:6, Paul says that the Spirit prompts us to cry out, "Abba! Father!" *Abba* was an Aramaic word, a term of family intimacy, used primarily by Jewish children when addressing their fathers. It implied a sense of child-like dependency but also of expectation that Abba would meet their needs. It was likewise the term Jesus used as he prayed to his Father in the Garden of Gethsemane.

Paul was apparently brought up in a strict Jewish family; in fact as an adult he became a Pharisee. As a small child, therefore, Paul would have addressed his father as Abba. So when he wants to express the deep intimacy believers enjoy with God, he reverts to this childhood word. Because he is writing to Greek-speaking Gentiles in Rome and Galatia, for clarity he adds the Greek word, *pateer*, which we translate as Father.

Stop and think about what this means. The One we are addressing is the sovereign creator, sustainer, and ruler of the entire universe. He is also infinitely holy in his moral purity. We, on the other hand, are dependent creatures who were dead in our trespasses and sins, and were enemies of God. How can we dare to address this sovereign and infinitely holy God as our Father? It is because we are in Christ, united to him in his sinless life and sin-bearing death. Christ is the one true Son of the Father, but because we are in him, God makes us his Sons also.

No other religion in the history of the world has ever had a god (or gods) who could be addressed in such intimate terms as Abba. Even the Jews of the Old

Testament who worshiped the one true God did not
address him as Father. And though there were notable
exceptions such as Abraham, Moses, David, and Daniel,
the vast majority of Jews did not enjoy an intimate relationship with God.

Opening the way. In the Old Testament era God
symbolically dwelt in the Most Holy Place of the taber-
nacle or temple. Only the High Priest could enter that
space, and even he could enter only once a year on the
Day of Atonement, and then only with the blood of the
sacrificial animal. So the Most Holy Place was guarded
by three restrictions (See Hebrews 9:7-8). Entrance to it
could only be made:

1. By the High Priest
2. Once a year
3. With the sacrificial blood

At the precise time of Christ's death on the cross, the
curtain separating the Most Holy Place from the holy
place was torn from top to bottom by the invisible hand of
God (Matthew 27:51). So now, under the New Covenant,
the first two restrictions in that list have been removed!

According to Hebrews 10:19-23, all of us now have
access to God. In fact, we are encouraged to draw near
to him, implying that our access is continual. The third
restriction, however, has not been removed, although it
has been changed. No longer do we come to the Father
with the blood of a sacrificial animal. We come by the
blood of Jesus himself. (Indeed, the blood of a sacrificial

animal was only ever sufficient under the Old Covenant because to God it represented and looked forward to the shed blood of Jesus.) So through Christ, more specifically through our *union* with Christ, we have continual and confident access to God, whom we may freely and rightly address as Father.

In coming to him, we come to one who sympathizes with our weaknesses and frailties. We come to "the throne of grace" where we may receive mercy and find grace to help in time of need (Hebrews 4:15, 16). We come to the one who says to us, "Cast all your anxieties on Me, because I care for you" (altered version of 1 Peter 5:7). We come to the one who says, "I will never leave you nor forsake you" (Hebrews 13:5). As we come, we may with the young Jewish children cry out "ABBA! FATHER!" expressing our dependence on him, and confidently, as little children, expecting him to hear us and to answer us according to his infinite wisdom and love.

Some readers may have problems with the treatment of God as our Father. Perhaps the behavior of their human fathers has made it more difficult for them to see God the Father as loving and benevolent. But the fact is, even the best of human fathers fall far, far short of the infinite perfection of our heavenly Father. True, God requires perfect obedience, but Jesus, as our representative, has already perfectly obeyed in our place. And now we stand before God as righteous as Jesus himself. This is true of all of us who have trusted in Christ as our Savior, whether we had a good human father or a difficult one.

Of course, if we are honest with ourselves, we see

so much sin still in our lives. And it seems the more we grow spiritually the more sin we see. And because we are performance-oriented by nature we tend to subjectively feel God's displeasure more than we do his loving, fatherly care. This means that, in order to experience the reality and full meaning of our adoption, we must also keep in mind our identity in Christ. This is how we counteract our own tendency to focus on our performance as a measure of God's acceptance. We must remind ourselves that God loves us, *not because we are loveable*, but *because we are in Christ*, and the love which the Father has for his Son flows over to us because we are in him.

There is an old hymn titled "A Child of the King," written by Harriet E. Buell (1834-1910). Sometimes when I feel discouraged about my Christian life, I sing to myself the words from the refrain, "I'm a child of the King," and it dashes my discouragement. Let me give you just one stanza of the hymn:

> I once was an outcast stranger on earth,
> A sinner by choice, and an alien by birth;
> But I've been adopted, my name's written down,
> An heir to a mansion, a robe, and a crown.

I am an adopted son of God. I'm a child of the King. I have the privilege in this life of an intimate father-child relationship with him, and I look forward with expectant hope to an eternal inheritance that is far more glorious than anything I can imagine.

Five
I AM A NEW CREATION

In considering our analogy of the serial killer and death row inmate pardoned and adopted by the governor, perhaps you thought to yourself, *There's something wrong with this picture. No one in his right mind would adopt and take into his home a serial killer.* Very true, yet in principle that is exactly what God did for us. How could that be?

Typically, if we are not actually murderers, felons, or adulterers, we tend to think of our common sins as no more serious than a parking violation. We are so used to living with pride, selfishness, envy, gossip, and a whole host of other "respectable sins" that we don't even think of them as sin.

But the fact is that, as serial sinners, we are all as guilty before God as that murderer. You and I sin every day in thought, word, deed, and motive. And whether those sins appear great or small in our own sight, in reality every sin we commit is an act of rebellion against God, a rejection and attempted negation of his sovereignty and rulership over us. And even more serious and damning than our countless individual acts of sin is the very fact of who we are apart from Christ. Through our representative union with Adam in his sin, we are all born serial sinners, sitting on death row awaiting eternal damnation.

The good news of the gospel is that Jesus took our place on God's death row and actually died in our place to satisfy the justice of God so that God might fully pardon us without violating his justice. But if all God did was pardon us, it would never make sense for him to bring us into his household as adopted children and heirs. That's why you may have thought to yourself, *How could the governor invite a death row inmate to live in his home? The man has the heart of killer!*

In the previous chapter we discussed two truths that follow from the analogy of that adopted murderer: in our adoption, we gain *an inheritance,* and we gain *a relationship* with God as our Father. But the third truth we must see is that, in pardoning and adopting us, God also does one other thing. He changes us into a different person, a new creation. As a result of being in Christ we are given a new heart, a new spirit, a new identity, and a new relationship.

A New Heart, a New Spirit

God has done for us what the governor could never do for the serial killer. He has radically changed our hearts, turning hearts of constant rebellion and disobedience to hearts fully capable of loving obedience.

Here is what God promised some six hundred years before the death of Christ.

> And I will give you a new heart, and a new spirit I
> will put within you. And I will remove the heart of
> stone from your flesh and give you a heart of flesh.
> And I will put my Spirit within you, and cause you to
> walk in my statutes and be careful to obey my rules
> (Ezekiel 36:26-27).

In this passage God promised two things: to radically change our hearts and to actually put his Holy Spirit within us to prompt us and enable us to obey God. The ultimate fulfillment of this promise awaits the new heaven and new earth when sin will be absolutely banished, but it has its beginnings in each of us the moment we trust in Christ as our Savior. That's why Paul could so confidently say: "Therefore, if anyone is in Christ, he is a new creation. The old has passed away; behold, the new has come (2 Corinthians 5:17).

There it is again, one of Paul's favorite expressions: "in Christ." It is only through our union with Christ that we can become a new creation. By the statement, "the old has passed away," Paul is referring to our old identity "in Adam." He says that this identity is completely gone; it is no longer our identity, no longer true of us. The best explanation for this is found in Romans 6:1-14.

A New Identity, a New Relationship

Romans 6 is admittedly difficult to understand, and over the last half-century commentators have written hundreds of pages about what they think Paul is saying.

I hold to what is probably the most generally accepted understanding of the chapter, the one that best explains why Paul's words, "the old has passed away," are true of us who are in Christ.

The occasion for Romans 6 is Paul's statement in Romans 5:20 that "Where sin increased, grace abounded all the more." He then anticipates a question, "Are we to continue in sin that grace may abound?" (Romans 6:1). His rather vigorous reply is, "By no means! How can we who died to sin still live in it?" (v 2). Here, Paul is not rebuking a cavalier attitude toward sin suggested by his question. Rather he is saying that a Christian continuing "in sin" is *impossible*. Why impossible? Because we died to sin through our union with Christ in his death (vv 6-8). We died to sin in that "our old self was crucified with him" (v 6), our "old self" being the person we were "in Adam."

In Adam, we were under both the *guilt of sin* and the *dominion of sin*. Under the dominion of sin, it was impossible for us to *obey* God. Under the guilt of sin it was impossible for us to *please* God. (See Romans 8:7-8.) But through our union with Christ in his death, we died to both sin's guilt and its dominion over us. We are now able to both obey and please God. Our old identity in Adam is gone, together with its bondage to the reign of sin.

So in writing, "By no means! How can we who died to sin still live in it?" Paul was not essentially saying, "How dare you imagine such a thing!" He was saying something more like, "Absolutely not. It can't possibly happen!" Yes, we may continue sinning—but we cannot possibly continue "in sin," because we are no longer "in

Adam." Paul is not issuing a moral rebuke. He is making an iron-clad theological statement.

When Paul says in 2 Corinthians 5:17 that the old has passed away, he is saying that our identity in Adam is gone forever. It's dead. The "new has come" refers to our new identity in Christ. We have a brand new relationship with God through Christ.

This identity is more than just a label. It defines who we really are. It means that God has taken away our stony hearts and given us hearts that are spiritually alive and responsive to him.

This categorical change, this transition from being in Adam to being in Christ is not something we could remotely have made happen on our own. God alone made it happen. The moment you trusted in Christ as Savior, the person you were in Adam *died*. You were *crucified with Christ*. You are now *in Christ*, and through that union with him the basic disposition of your heart has been changed. That is why God can take you into his spiritual family, adopting you as his own.

A New Way to Live

But Romans 6 is also about more than theology. Paul is not content to leave us with theory. He wants us to act on this radical change in our identity by applying the truth of it to our everyday lives. So he says in verse 11, "So you also must consider yourselves dead to sin and alive to God in Christ Jesus." The word *consider* that Paul uses here is best understood as meaning "think about carefully, especially with regard to taking action."

Paul wants us to see that through our union with Christ Jesus, we not only have been delivered from the dominion and bondage of sin, we also have been united to Jesus in his life—we are both dead to sin and alive to God. We are branches on the vine that is Christ, and because of this we partake of the spiritual life and vitality that is in him.

This is the meaning of "the new has come" in 2 Corinthians 5:17. In Romans 6, Paul is saying all this "newness" is a settled, established, and unchangeable fact, but at the same time something we must continually think about and act on. That is why, in Romans 6:12, he immediately adds an action step: "Let not sin therefore reign in your mortal body, to make you obey its passions" (v 12). After all, one might reasonably ask: "If we have truly been delivered from the dominion of sin, if it no longer rules us, why must we be diligent not to let sin reign in our mortal bodies? What difference does it really make?"

The New Testament is very clear. It makes a huge difference. You and I are now engaged in a spiritual guerilla warfare against remaining corruption within us, and that warfare has real consequences—for ourselves, others, and the glory of God—depending on how we engage in it. This warfare is described by Paul in Galatians 5:17, "For the desires of the flesh are against the Spirit, and the desires of the Spirit are against the flesh, for these are opposed to each other, to keep you from doing the things you want to do."

Though we have been delivered from absolute bondage to sin, we have not been freed from its presence or influence. And as long as sin is present within us, it will seek to regain its dominion over us. While sin can never fully succeed at this, it can make life far more difficult, far more painful, and far less fruitful.

Here is a flawed but possibly helpful analogy. Think of a prisoner of war camp. Suppose the POWs have somehow managed to overcome their guards, confiscate their weapons and have set out to engage in guerilla warfare against their enemy. They are freed from the bondage they were under as prisoners, but they are still in enemy territory and are very much in danger from their former captors. So they must be alert and diligent in their efforts to evade their enemy, and they must be prepared to engage in defensive action when necessary.

We have an enemy that does not stop opposing us. To live as if this were not true is simply foolish. We are freed from sin's dominion, but it still desires to destroy us. So we must be vigilant against its assaults, and take steps by God's Spirit to put to death the expressions of sin that we see daily in our bodies and minds (see Romans 8:13).

Paul wants us to remember that, since we are freed from bondage to sin, we can say No to temptations. Only in eternity will it be *impossible* for us to sin, but for now it is always possible for us *not* to sin in response to specific temptations. We may choose to sin, and we often do choose to sin, but we do not *have to* sin.

When we were in Adam, and thus under sin's dominion, we had no choice but to sin at every temptation. Obviously, this is not to say, for example, that every time an unsaved person is tempted to adultery, he or she commits adultery. But it is to say that every time an unsaved person is tempted to sin in some way, some sin is committed in response. But once we are in Christ, we are able to say No to sin, and that is an ability we simply did not have prior to our conversion, because we were in Adam.

The fact that we have died to the dominion of sin is not a truth to be put on a shelf and admired. It is a truth we must put to use every day.

When We Fail

Sad to say, we often do not take advantage of our new identity in Christ. As we saw in Galatians 5:17, the flesh continues to strive against the Spirit, and it frequently gets the upper hand in our lives. So what should we do then? The answer is that we take that sin to the cross and remember that Jesus died for the very sin of which we are now ashamed. Furthermore, in the very temptation where we sinned, Jesus obeyed in his humanity. He was tempted in all points as we are, yet was without sin.

That's why it's important to consider yourselves dead to sin and alive to God in Christ Jesus—that is, to count on the fact that in Christ's death, we died not only to sin's dominion but also to its guilt. Because Jesus fully satisfied the justice of God toward our sin, God no longer counts it against us.

But what about our struggles with persistent sin patterns, when we are tempted to feel that we have exhausted the patience and forgiveness of God? We should still bring that sin to the cross in an attitude of repentance and contrition, knowing and believing that there is no sin that is beyond the cleansing power of the blood of Christ. As God said in Isaiah 1:18, "though your sins are like scarlet, they shall be as white as snow; though they are red like crimson, they shall become as wool." We cannot resist the power of remaining sin in our lives if we have not first dealt with its guilt. And the only way to do this is to continually go back to the cross and see Jesus bearing that sin and paying its penalty through his death.

We truly are new creations in Christ. The old person we were in Adam has passed away. The new person we are in Christ has come. Yet it often seems as if the old person we were in Adam is still very much alive. But that is not our true identity. It is the flesh striving against the Spirit. Our true identity is in Christ. And through his power applied to us by the Holy Spirit we can make progress in becoming new creations in our daily experience as well as in our identity.

Examine Yourselves

But there is a sober note to this truth. Do we indeed show evidence of being new creations in Christ? The apostle Paul's words to the Corinthians apply to us also: "Examine yourselves, to see whether you are in the faith. Test yourselves. Or do you not realize this about your-selves, that Jesus Christ is in you?--unless indeed you fail to meet the test!" (2 Corinthians 13:5). Here are some questions to help us examine ourselves:

- What is my attitude toward God? Do I gladly ac-knowledge my dependence on him and my account-ability to him?

- What is my attitude toward my sin? Am I concerned or indifferent about it?
- What is my attitude toward Jesus Christ? Do I trust in him as the one who died for my sin on the cross?
- What is my attitude toward the Bible? Do I truly want to grow in my understanding and application of it in my life?
- What is my attitude toward prayer? Do I also want to grow in this area of my life, or am I quite content to see prayer as an occasional call out to God for help?
- What is my attitude toward other Christians? Do I appreciate being with them and learning from them, or do I actually prefer the company and lifestyle of my non-Christian friends?

These are important questions that we should seek to answer truthfully. The stakes are too high to ignore them or play games with them. Our eternal destiny is at stake and eternity lasts forever. There is no end to it. All of us will spend eternity in the blessed presence of God, or we will spend it under the never-ending curse and wrath of God.

So the question each of us should honestly face is this: Do I have some evidence that I am a new creation? Can we say something such as this: Yes, I still struggle with remaining sin and I see my frequent failures, but as I look at these questions I can truthfully say that, though I have a long way to go, I believe I'm headed in the right direction.

Having examined ourselves, we should also be

concerned for friends and relatives who consider themselves to be Christians, but who show little or no evidence of being new creations. At the very least we should pray that God will lead them to a genuine saving knowledge of Christ. And then, depending on our relationship with them, we can seek to graciously challenge them to examine themselves.

Privilege and Responsibility

I said in the introduction to this book that our identity in Christ involves both privilege and responsibility. That is certainly true with respect to the subject matter of this chapter.

Privilege. Our positions of being justified, adopted, and a new creation in Christ are ours, but they are basically privileges. God has done it all through Christ. We who used to be in Adam — with our guilt and bondage to sin — have died, having been crucified with Christ. We are now alive unto God through his Spirit who dwells within us. We do not have to sin. We can say No to temptations from our flesh, the world, or the devil.

Responsibility. Our right and proper response is to believe these truths about ourselves, rejoice in them, and live in the reality of them. We must not let sin reign in our bodies (Romans 6:12). When we do allow sin to get the upper hand we must immediately confess it, repent of it, and take it to the cross to experience the cleansing power of the blood of Christ. We cannot deal with the power of sin unless we have first dealt with its guilt. And we deal with it at the cross.

I am a new creation, with a new heart, a new spirit, and a new identity before God. Having been delivered from the dominion of sin and united to Christ, I am always able to resist temptation. When I do sin, I am always welcome at the cross, for all my sins have been forgiven in Jesus.

Six
I AM A SAINT

Saint is one of the most widely misunderstood words in our Christian vocabulary. At some point in church history, people began to call the original apostles saints, contrary to the plain meaning of the word as used in the New Testament. So now we hear of Saint Paul, Saint Peter, Saint Andrew, and the like. In the Roman Catholic tradition, people of unusual achievement are sometimes designated as saints. Among evangelicals we often think of saints as exceptionally godly and holy people.

The truth is, though, every believer is a saint. That's why Paul's greetings in his epistles often include something such as, "To the saints who are in Ephesus," (Ephesians 1:1, see also Philippians 1:1, Colossians 1:2). Even when addressing Corinth, a church that was all messed up both theologically and morally, Paul wrote, "To the church of God that is in Corinth, to those sancti-fied in Christ Jesus, called to be saints…" (1 Corinthians 1:2). In fact, sainthood is not a spiritual attainment, or even a recognition of such attainment. It is rather a state or status into which God brings every believer. All Chris-tians are saints.

It is a very unfortunate and unhelpful thing that we so often misunderstand this short, simple word. To use a word that applies to *all* Christians in a way that suggests there is a special, elite *class* of Christians, is doubly wrong: it steals from the church important truths that God intended to communicate through the idea of sainthood, and it promotes jealousy and division within the body of Christ by suggesting a hierarchy that does not exist.

Let's see what being a saint really means.

Christ's Own Possession

Closely associated with *saint* are the words *sanctify* and *sanctification*. All three words are from the same Greek word family (*hagios, hagiasmos* and *hagiazo*). That's why Paul writes to the Corinthians as "those sanctified in Christ Jesus, called to be saints." So a saint is someone who has been sanctified. If you have been a believer for a while, you may be thinking, *But isn't sanctification a process, the process of becoming more holy?* Yes, but that's not all it is.

The basic meaning of the verb *sanctify* is "to separate or set apart." A saint is someone who has been set apart. Set apart for what? A better question is, "Set apart for whom?" And the answer is, for God.

Both Paul and Peter use an identical phrase to refer to Christians: "a people for his own possession" (Titus 2:14, 1 Peter 2:9). Paul says, "Christ, who gave himself for us.... to purify for himself a people for his own possession." Peter says, "But you are a chosen race, a royal priesthood, a holy nation, a people for his own possession." This phrase gets at the heart of what it means to be a saint. We have been set apart to be Christ's own possession.

This is the language of ownership. As saints we no longer "own" ourselves in the sense that we are free to live as we please. Rather, as Paul says in 1 Corinthians 6:19-20, "You are not your own, for you were bought with a price." A saint is someone who no longer belongs to or "owns" himself. The name on the title to his life is no longer the name he is known by. The titleholder to the life of every Christian is Jesus Christ. This is what it means for Christ to be Lord.

We speak often of the Lordship of Christ over our lives. Indeed, the prayer I most often pray for our grandchildren is that they will trust Christ as their Savior and obey him as Lord. So Lordship is a good term, but we might understand it better if we sometimes spoke of Lordship for what it truly is: Christ's ownership over our lives.

In today's Christian culture, this is actually a radical concept, if not an outright offensive one. We regularly talk about how we may choose to *give* something to God. I *give* some of *my* time or *my* money. The clear implication of this kind of language is not only that all my possessions are my own, but that I, too, belong entirely to myself, and I go through life making choices about how I will invest my time, my energy, and my resources.

The Bible has an entirely different perspective: none of these things are your own. Indeed, you are not your own. You were bought with a price, the price being the blood of the Son of God shed for your salvation. Having been purchased, you no longer belong to yourself.

I'm not suggesting that you have to ask the Lord's permission to make every little daily decision about how to spend your time and money. No, God has given us a great deal of freedom in our decisions and choices (see for example Romans 14:1-12). But I am suggesting that probably all of us should become more thoughtful about whether our actions and decisions are pleasing to our "owner," the Lord Jesus Christ. The Scripture says, "So, whether you eat or drink, or whatever you do, do all to the glory of God" (1 Corinthians 10:31). Whatever I do, I am to do it for God's glory. This includes all of life.

Note, for example, Paul's words to the slaves in the Colossian church, "Whatever you do, work heartily, as for the Lord and not for men,... You are serving the Lord Christ" (Colossians 3:23). Although Paul was addressing slaves, the principle behind his words applies equally to employer-employee relationships. Let's say you are a promising young executive in a large corporation. As you aspire to greater responsibility and commensurate salary increases, why are you doing it? In this context, who is the practical owner of your life? Is it you, or Christ? Do you desire that promotion for your benefit, or for Christ's glory? This is just one example, but the principle applies to all of life. Our whole outlook on life should be colored by the fact that, as saints, we no longer belong to ourselves, but to him.

The Work of the Holy Spirit

The more common and actually erroneous view of *saint* is that it is some kind of second step in the Christian life.

Those who want to "go all out" in being a Christian, if they try really hard, can become the kind of person some might call a "saint." For Christians who hold that view, the straightforward biblical definition of *saint* that I'm trying to communicate comes off as odd or radical when in fact it is an essential, inescapable aspect of the gospel. Indeed, this being "set apart" by the work of the Holy Spirit to be Christ's own possession is at the very center of our salvation experience. Consider the following two passages:

> But we ought always to give thanks to God for you, brothers beloved by the Lord, because God chose you as the firstfruits to be saved, through sanctification by the Spirit and belief in the truth. To this he called you through our gospel, so that you may obtain the glory of our Lord Jesus Christ. (2 Thessalonians 2:13-14)

> Peter, an apostle of Jesus Christ, To those who are elect exiles of the dispersion in Pontus, Galatia, Cappadocia, Asia, and Bithynia, according to the foreknowledge of God the Father, in the sanctification of the Spirit, for obedience to Jesus Christ and for sprinkling with his blood: May grace and peace be multiplied to you. (1 Peter 1:1-2)

Note that in these two passages both Peter and Paul connect the sanctifying work of the Spirit to our salvation. In the New International Version, 2 Thessalonians 2:13 reads, "God chose you to be saved through the sanctify-

ing work of the Spirit and through belief in the truth."
And 1 Peter 1:2 reads, "[You] have been chosen according
to the foreknowledge of God the Father, through the
sanctifying work of the Spirit, for obedience to Jesus
Christ and sprinkling by his blood."

We see in both of these passages that the sanctifying work of the Spirit, far from being a second step in the
Christian life, is actually *the first step*. It is because of the
setting-apart work of the Spirit that we actually do believe
the truth of the gospel and trust in Christ as our Savior.

- We were dead in our sins, but he made us alive
  (Ephesians 2:1, 4).
- We were under the power of Satan, but he rescued us
  (Acts 26:18).
- We were in the domain of darkness but he delivered
  us (Colossians 1:13).
- Our minds were blinded by Satan, but he opened
  them to the truth (2 Corinthians 4:4-5).

Yes, we believe the gospel, but we do so because the
Spirit has set us apart to be Christ's own possession. Yes,
we do obey Jesus Christ by trusting in him, but we do
so because of the setting-apart work of the Holy Spirit.
There is no salvation apart from God's sanctifying work.

When we return to one of our earlier verses, 1 Corinthians 1:2, we see also that we are sanctified in Christ Jesus.
Remember that "in Christ" is Paul's shorthand expression
for our union with Christ. So the work of the Spirit is to
unite us to Christ, both as our representative before God

in his sinless life and his death, and also as the source of our new spiritual life as we are grafted into the vine. This means that the sanctifying work of the Spirit is more than merely a change of labels such as from sinner to saint. It is a change of heart. Therefore it must express itself, though in varying degrees, in everyone who trusts in Christ as Savior. This thought naturally leads to the next subject.

Progressive Sanctification

It is the nature of life, whether in a plant, an animal, or a human being, to grow to a stage of maturity. The same is true of the spiritual life we have from God, with a major difference that we never fully arrive at spiritual maturity in this life. This spiritual growth has historically been called *sanctification*. However, in order to distinguish it from the point-in-time sanctification by the Spirit that has been the theme of this chapter so far, some of us use the term *progressive sanctification*. In this phrase, *progressive* implies progress or growth, and this theme appears repeatedly in the New Testament letters. There is no question about it. We are to pursue spiritual maturity.

Scores of books have been written on progressive sanctification, including several by me. So it is well beyond the scope of this chapter to discuss this subject except to make two observations.

- The definitive point-in-time sanctification that makes us "saints" is solely the work of the Holy Spirit. We contribute nothing to his divine almighty action. In this sanctification we are all equally sanctified.

- By contrast, progressive sanctification involves our utmost effort, though that effort must be directed and empowered by the Holy Spirit. This sanctification varies in degree from one believer to another, and as I stated earlier, will never be completed in this life.

The Motivation for Living as a Saint

The implications of living as a saint—one who is "owned" by Christ Jesus—are quite radical, far more so than most of us are accustomed to thinking about. What then will motivate us to pursue saintly lives? What is it that will make us *want* to be what we *ought* to be? The answer is love and gratitude for what God has done for us in Christ, as expressed in the gospel.

Jesus once said to a self-righteous Pharisee, "he who is forgiven little, loves little" (Luke 7:47). The opposite is obviously true. He who is forgiven much, loves much. The question for each of us then is, how much do we realize we've been forgiven? If we define sin largely in terms of the more flagrant sins that we don't commit, then we will have little sense of our own sin, and little sense of forgiveness, and consequently little love for Christ.

But if we truly grasp the idea that being a saint means being one of Christ's own possessions, and if we acknowledge how far short we come in living up to that reality, then we will begin to see how much we've been forgiven. And the good news of the gospel is that we truly have been forgiven of the sin of living largely for ourselves, that is, of effectively stealing the ownership of our loves from Christ.

After spending three quarters of his letter to the Romans on the mercies of God as displayed in the gospel, Paul says, "I appeal to you therefore, brothers, by the mercies of God, to present your bodies as a living sacrifice, holy and acceptable to God, which is your spiritual worship" (Romans 12:1). In effect Paul is appealing to them, and to us, to acknowledge Christ's ownership by presenting our bodies, or our entire selves to him as a continual daily living sacrifice. But we are to do so *in view of the mercies of God*. Our love and gratitude can only be a response to his love and mercy toward us.

So once again we see that our identity in Christ, our answer to the question "Who am I?" involves both privileges and responsibilities. Though in this chapter we've focused more on the responsibilities, consider the inestimable privilege of being a saint. We *have been* delivered from the power of Satan, we *have been* freed from the domain of darkness, our minds which were blinded by Satan *have been* opened to understand and believe the gospel. All this is bound up in the action of the Holy Spirit in setting us apart to be Christ's possession.

I am a saint: I do not belong to myself, but to God. I have been purchased and declared holy by God, and set apart for God. Thus, God is ever at work to cause me to grow in spiritual maturity, a process in which he calls me to cooperate, in every way, out of gratitude for his mercy.

Seven
I AM A SERVANT OF CHRIST

In his letter to the Romans, Paul introduces himself as "Paul, a servant of Christ Jesus, called to be an apostle, set apart for the gospel of God" (Romans 1:1). In this chapter we will use Paul's three-part self-description as our topical outline. We will see that:

- We are all servants of Christ Jesus.
- We all have a divine calling from God to serve others in a particular role or roles.
- We may eventually recognize that within our calling we have been set apart by God for a particular area of focus or specialty.

Servants

The word translated *servant* that Paul used in Romans 1:1 literally means *slave*. Most of us associate slavery with the way it was practiced in the United States. But slavery in the Roman culture was not nearly as harsh or demeaning. For our understanding, therefore, *servant* is probably a better rendering of the word overall. We should also remember, however, that although slaves in Roman times were allowed to purchase their freedom, and many did, during the time they were slaves they were actually owned by their masters. In that sense, they were in a position similar to us, as we are "owned" by Christ Jesus.

If Paul begins his self-description by calling himself a servant of Christ, we should ask ourselves what he means by that statement. The answer is that Paul served Christ as he served others in the context of his calling.

It's easy for us to imagine that in serving others through his ministry, Paul was genuinely serving Christ. But what about the vast majority of us who will never make any portion of our living from direct gospel service? As he goes about his work, can a Christian plumber say, "I am a servant of Christ"? Can a computer programmer, or a chef, or a bookkeeper? Paul gives us the answer to all such questions as he addresses slaves in Colossians 3:22-24.

> Slaves, obey in everything those who are your earthly masters, not by way of eye-service, as people-pleasers, but with sincerity of heart, fearing the Lord. Whatever you do, work heartily, as for the Lord and not for men, knowing that from the Lord you will receive the inheritance as your reward. You are serving the Lord Christ.

Note the three references to the Lord. The slaves were to work with sincerity, *fearing the Lord*. They were to work heartily, *as for the Lord*. And then Paul says, "You are serving the Lord Christ." The slaves were to serve Christ through serving their masters. Any legitimate vocational pursuit can be pursued in this very same way. Anyone pursuing a calling from God can and should see himself or herself every bit a servant of Christ Jesus as was Paul the apostle.

Sad to say, I think very few Christians see their temporal vocations or professions in this way. They may be conscientious and desirous of doing their best, but they do not see themselves as servants of Christ in their work. They intuitively think only of those in vocational Christian work as serving Christ.

This was true of my own life when I was serving as a young navy officer, and later when I was working in manufacturing. I tried to do the best job I could, but I never thought of myself as serving Christ by serving my country or by serving the customers of my company. In fact, when I was working in industry, I was also serving voluntarily in the Navigators ministry, and it was only when engaged in some ministry activity that I thought of myself as "serving the Lord."

The goal of this book, with its several answers to the question "Who am I?" is to help us find that our true identity is to be found only in Christ in all the various relationships that we have to him. Just as every believer is a saint, so every believer is, like Paul, a servant of Christ Jesus. This certainly includes our identity in the area that, for many people, consumes forty to sixty hours of their week.

What does it look like to serve Christ in the secular workplace? One of my favorite illustrations answering that question is from a retired automobile salesman. He had sold cars most of his adult life. At some point in that career he had trusted Christ as Savior. He said to me, "Before I became a Christian, I sold cars. After I became a Christian, I helped people buy cars."

This man was telling me that, before becoming a Christian he was not concerned about the desires and needs of the potential buyer, but only about the commission he would receive if he sold the car. Likely he would try to sell more expensive cars because of the larger commission. But after he became a Christian, his primary interest was to help the potential customer find the best car for his needs and his budget. His motivation changed from serving himself to serving his customer. He had learned to serve Christ by serving people. I love this true story because it so beautifully makes the point that we can serve Christ by serving people, even in a business not particularly noted for that attitude.

What about those whose jobs do not bring them into contact with people outside of their work place? Consider, for example, the many office workers who never see anyone who benefits from their company's products or services. How can these men and women serve Christ by serving people? In seeking to do consistently high quality work, believing that God will bless their efforts, and trusting that God is pleased with their work for the benefit of their company, they are ultimately serving Christ by serving the customers of that company. These are all ways in ways in which Christ is served through our service to others.

We serve Christ by serving people. We may be serving employers, customers, clients, patients, or even co-workers. Whoever it may be that we have an opportunity to serve, whatever our job or profession might be, we should see ourselves first as servants of Christ, and second, as members of our profession or work group.

If you make part of your identity, "I am a servant of Christ," then at the end of the week, instead of saying, "Thank goodness it's Friday," you can say, "This week I had the privilege of serving Christ by serving people."

As Christians, we really are servants of Christ far more so than we are employees — or for that matter, more so than we are spouses, children, or retirees. Every one of us should have an image in our minds of our real "business card":

[Your name here]
Servant of Jesus Christ

Called

The second part of Paul's self-description is that he is "called" — in his particular case, "called to be an apostle." The verb *called* is passive, indicating there is someone who performed the calling. Obviously that someone is God, so Paul is saying that he has been called by God to be an apostle.

The Roman slaves to whom Paul likens himself in Romans 1:1 always had a job in the master's household.

The jobs varied from menial tasks to roles of significant responsibility. So when Paul introduces himself as a servant of Christ Jesus, he has in mind his calling—the specific job, or role, assigned to him. We know this because he continues to express himself in terms of his office and role as one called and purchased by God.

People in full-time Christian work today also speak of being called to their ministry. A minister—whether in a church or the mission field or a para-church ministry—should believe with a high level of confidence that he or she has been called by God to that position. I can tell you, for example, when and how God called me to serve with the Navigators.

Of course, ministers today understand that we are not called to be apostles as Paul and the twelve (including Matthias) were. Their calling was unique. God called them to be the founders of the New Testament church and the authors, either directly or indirectly, of all the New Testament. No one today has the authority or the divine guidance that they had. Nevertheless, in a more limited sense ministers are legitimately and actually called by God to his service.

Once again we must ask, "But what about those of us not active in vocational ministry?" Can we say that we are "called" by God to our particular role? For example, can the Christian physician say, "I am in this career because God has called me to it?" I believe the answer is yes, for three essential reasons.

If the Christian who is not a minister cannot claim that God has called him to his role:

1. It strips non-ministerial vocations of the inherent dignity that God endowed them with when he ordained work in the Garden of Eden.

2. It creates a huge group of second-class citizens in the kingdom of God. The Bible does teach that in eternity not all believers will be rewarded to the same degree. However, those distinctions will not be based on *what* role we were called to serve in, but on *how* we served in the position to which we were called (e.g., Revelation 22:12, 1 Corinthians 3:14-15).

3. It radically undercuts the concept of God's providence—his directing and orchestrating of events and circumstances that seem to "point" us in a particular vocational direction. It suggests that calling someone to be a bus driver instead of a pastor, for example, is somehow a lesser expression of God's perfect wisdom, knowledge, and power. It is not.

At the same time, we can identify at least one common difference in the sense of calling. The call to a non-ministerial vocation typically comes in the form of God's providential guidance by which he brings together interests, strengths, and opportunities to "open doors" in such a way that walking through them is mostly a matter of wise judgment. In a call to church or para-church ministry, however, there is often present to a more marked degree a subjective element involving the person's perception of God's will. It may be something from Scripture that gets one's attention, or it may be the "still small voice" of a thought in the mind, or perhaps a growing conviction that God is calling one. However the call comes, it must be subjectively evaluated and responded to.

In Psalms 139:16, David said, "in your book were written, every one of them, the days that were formed for me, when as yet there was none of them." David was saying, "God had a plan for me before I was born, which he will execute day-by-day throughout my life." What was true of David is true for all of us. God has ordained some to be auto mechanics, some to be teachers, and some to be missionaries, and he will so arrange the circumstances and events of our lives that we will end up in the vocation to which he has called us.

I believe, therefore, that every Christian should have the privilege of saying, "I've been called of God to this particular vocation, and I am here to serve Jesus Christ by serving people." This should be just as true of the custodian at the local elementary school as it is of a world-acclaimed heart surgeon, or a pioneer missionary serving in some remote area of the world. Such thinking can and should give a sense of dignity to our work, whatever it is. It can and should motivate us to do our jobs as best as we can, and give us the perseverance to keep going when the work is difficult or unrewarding.

Finally, in this matter of calling, there is the service of every Christian in the body of Christ. First Peter 4:10 says, "As each has received a gift, use it to serve one another, as good stewards of God's varied grace." Taken in context, Peter is telling us that every believer has a spiritual gift with which to serve in the local church or other ministries. We can think of this as a function or a role to play in the body. Christ has purchased every aspect of our life, and as such we belong to him not only with respect to our life in the larger society, but obviously with respect to our life in the body of Christ. God rules over our lives in each of these spheres.

The idea that each of us has a spiritual gift to use within the body is generally accepted among evangelical Christians, but it is not often emphasized. As a result we have large numbers of "consumer Christians," people who are not involved beyond Sunday church attendance, and who therefore cannot honestly identify themselves as "servants of Christ Jesus" in the spiritual dimension of their lives. It is beyond the scope of this book to treat this subject in detail, but suffice it to say that all I have said about serving Christ and our calling in the daily workplace applies in principle to the exercise of our spiritual gifts in the body.

Determining one's spiritual gift typically involves a process of "trying on" different roles such as teaching, administration, hospitality, and mercy. But certainly every Christian, with the possible exception of those who are young or new in the faith, should have the privilege of being able to say, "I know what my spiritual gift is, and by God's grace, I am able to exercise it."

Set Apart

The third expression Paul uses to introduce himself is that he is "set apart for the gospel of God." He could be using this expression simply as a clarification of the word *apostle* — which would then be true of all the apostles — or he could be using it to emphasize the unique ministry God had given *him* as an apostle. I think it was the latter, for this reason: Paul was given his understanding of the gospel by direct revelation from Christ (Galatians 1:11-16), and he was given the task of explaining it clearly, as he does in Romans. Most of what we believe about the gospel today, and for that matter, most of what we know about our identity in Christ, comes from the pen of the apostle Paul. So I think Paul viewed his role as an apostle to be one of proclaiming, explaining, and defending the gospel, and that he was *set apart* for that special purpose.

What is the relevance of this to us today? Just this: someday you may find that you have been set apart by God for a specific task or role beyond the general category of your calling. I joined the Navigators staff in 1955 as a trainee. I assumed that after a year or two I would be sent overseas as a missionary. But after about a year, I was asked to become part of the administrative staff. I spent the next thirty-eight years serving in various administrative roles. So I can say that I was called to be a staff member in the Navigators, and was set apart for administration. During the last fifteen of those thirty-eight years I was spending more and more time in a teaching ministry, until in 1994 I transitioned completely into writing and teaching. Now I would say that I have been set apart specifically to be a Bible teacher within the Navigators.

I have a friend who was called by God to be in the insurance business and who eventually became a top executive in his company. He was the broker for the Navigators property and liability insurance, as well as for the insurance of several other Christian organizations. Some years ago he called together those of us who were responsible for insurance in our respective organizations and urged us to join together to form our own "captive" insurance company, in the same way large companies do. We did this with his coaching and his company's assistance with the legal and financial issues.

During the first ten years of the new insurance company's operation, the Navigators saved more than a million dollars, and other organizations the company served had similar results. This concept was so successful that a number of other Christian organizations and churches have now formed a second such company.

My friend retired several years ago, and all the member organizations of our company held a dinner to honor him. Even though I was no longer directly involved, I was invited to give a short talk of appreciation. I used Romans 1:1 as an outline of my talk. I said this man was a servant of Christ whom God had *called* to be in the insurance industry, and that at the proper time God had *set him apart* to pioneer the concept of captive insurance companies among Christian organizations. This had all begun many years earlier when, as an insurance executive, he sought to serve Christ by serving the companies that looked to him for their insurance coverage.

Someday you, too, may find that God has set you apart for a more specific purpose. Perhaps it has already happened. I encourage you to see this as part and parcel of your calling in God, and also as a special expression of your service to Christ through serving others.

In closing this chapter, I must note one more reason for referring to ourselves as servants rather than "slaves." In the Old Testament era, leaders of the people such as Moses, Joshua, and David were called, "Servant of the Lord" (Joshua 14:7, 24:29; Psalms 89:3). The phrase was a title of honor, and we should esteem it in that same way today. *Servant* is thus an essential part of our identity, an essential part of who we are in Christ Jesus. We are servants of the One who is Lord of lords and King of kings (Revelation 17:14).

I am a servant of Jesus Christ. By God's grace, I serve him by serving others in the particular role or roles to which, in his providential wisdom, he has called me.

Eight
I AM NOT YET PERFECT

There is yet one more truth to grapple with as we seek to realize our true identity in Christ. That is the obvious tension between who we are in Christ and what we see ourselves to be in our daily lives.

The apostle Paul, in the context of wanting to know Christ more and be like him said, "Not that I have already obtained this or am already perfect" (Philippians 3:12). Surely all of us can identify with Paul and say, "I am not yet perfect."

The Tension of an Unfinished Life

We live in the era between the coming of the Holy Spirit on the day of Pentecost and the second coming of Jesus himself, an era described by theologians as "already, but not yet." There is then a tension between what we already are through our identity in Christ, and what we see ourselves to be in our daily experience.

- In Christ we stand perfectly righteous before God, but in our daily lives, we see much remaining sin.
- In Christ we are adopted sons of God, but in our experience we sometimes feel like orphans.
- In Christ we are new creations, but it does not always seem as if "the old has passed away."

If we are going to grow in our realization of who we are in Christ, then we must learn to live with the tension of *not* being in our daily experience what we *are* in Christ.

Paul seemed to exult in this tension. Not that he rejoiced in his remaining imperfection. Rather, he rejoiced in the contrast between who he was in himself and who he was in Christ. He saw that his remaining imperfection *magnified the grace of God.* To paraphrase 1 Corinthians 15:9-10, Paul said, "I am not worthy to be an apostle, but I am an apostle by the grace of God." In Ephesians 3:8 he wrote, "To me, though I am the very least of all the saints, this grace was given, to preach to the Gentiles the unsearchable riches of Christ." And finally near the end of his life he could say, "Christ Jesus came into the world to save sinners, of whom I am the foremost" (1 Timothy 1:15).

This is how Paul viewed himself—not only the least of the apostles, but the very least of all God's people (the saints), and in fact the foremost of sinners—*but he did so in order to magnify the contrast between who he was in himself and who he was in Christ.* If you and I are going to make progress in realizing who we are in Christ, we must openly and honestly face who we are in ourselves; we are not yet perfect, we still sin daily in thought, word, deed, and motive. In fact, on some days we sin miserably.

Our tendency, however, is to look *within ourselves* to try to find some reason to feel good *about ourselves*, and this, of course, misses the point entirely. We are performance-oriented by nature, that is, by our sinful nature. To use a British term, we don't want to be "on the dole" — to be a charity case before God. We want to "pay our own way" to self-respect based on what we accomplish.

In the introduction to this book I mentioned a woman with a broken marriage who had said to a mutual friend, "I am just a failure." I did not add that the man had responded to her by saying kindly, "No, you are not a failure." When I heard that part of the story, I winced and thought, *Oh, I wish you hadn't said that.*

My friend was trying to prop up the lady's self-esteem. But that is always a futile effort, an exercise in misplaced compassion. You can't deny reality, and the fact was that this woman had failed in her marriage. But there was another, greater reality. Because this woman is a believer, the greater reality was and is that, as one in Christ, she stands holy and blameless before God (Ephesians 1:4). That is why I wish my friend had said something like, "You are right. You are a failure, and so am I. But that's why Jesus came. He came to die for failures like you and me. Because of Jesus, our failures no longer define who we truly are."

If we are to grow in the realization of who we are in Christ we must keep the gospel continually before us. To use an expression I heard in the 1980s, "We must preach the gospel to ourselves every day." We must believe that God forgives and welcomes sinners. As the Puritan Thomas

Wilcox said, "In all the Scripture there is not one hard word against a poor sinner stripped of his self-righteousness."

Sinners Embraced

When a family has "skeletons in the closet," it can mean they have some particularly disreputable ancestors. As the expression suggests, families usually try to keep these things hidden. Well, Jesus in his humanity had some skeletons in his closet, but it's fascinating to note that, rather than hiding these connections, the Bible goes to unusual lengths to emphasize them.

Consider the genealogy of Jesus as recorded in Matthew 1:1-16. To begin with, four women are mentioned. That is unusual because women were not usually included in the biblical genealogies. What's more, all four of these women had significant immoral baggage in their histories.

- Matthew 1:3 – Tamar, the daughter-in-law of Judah, disguised herself as a prostitute and committed incest with Judah.
- Matthew 1:5 – Rahab is clearly identified as a prostitute. See Hebrews 11:31.
- Matthew 1:5 – Ruth, though a virtuous woman herself, was a Moabite. The Moabite tribe originated as a result of incest between drunken Lot and one of his daughters. Later, Moabite women committed immorality with the Israelite men when they were in the wilderness.
- Matthew 1:6 – Bathsheba had committed adultery with David

Three of the men in Jesus' genealogy didn't look so good either.

- Jacob was a deceiver, yet in Luke 1:33 the angel said to Mary, "he will reign over the house of Jacob forever."
- Judah was an immoral man, yet in Revelation 5:5 Jesus is called "the Lion of the tribe of Judah."
- David committed adultery with Bathsheba and orchestrated the death of her husband, yet in Luke 1:32 the angel Gabriel said, "the Lord God will give to [Jesus] the throne of his father David."

So Jesus had plenty of skeletons in the closet of his genealogy. And Matthew, writing under the divine guidance of the Holy Spirit, does not hesitate to mention them. In fact, he seems to make a point of doing so. What's going on here? What is the Holy Spirit saying to us through these skeletons in the closet?

Jesus identified with and understood sinners. He identified with sinners in his genealogy. He identified with tax collectors and sinners during his life (Mark 2:15). He identified with the thief at his death and said to him, "Truly, I say to you, today you will be with me in Paradise" (Luke 23:43).

Yes, Jesus identified with sinners, and this is good news for us, because we are still sinners—saved sinners to be sure, but we remain sinners nevertheless in our daily lives. And Jesus loves us despite our sin, and sits at the right hand of the Father interceding for us (Romans 8:34).

Grace Trumps Performance

I mentioned in chapter three how we all have good days and bad days. The point is well worth making again, for our daily struggle against sin continually drives us to measure our acceptance before God on the basis of our performance.

On a good day we may get out of bed as soon as the alarm goes off and have a refreshing quiet time. Events of the day generally fall out the right way and we encounter no significant sin issues. A bad day is just the opposite. We oversleep, skip our quiet time, muddle through a difficult day, and struggle all day long with sinful thoughts (resentment, envy, frustration, lust, etc.). On which of those days would you be more expectant of God's blessing or answers to prayer? Your answer to that question reveals whether you are living by your works, or by the gospel.

Our default setting is to live by our works. But let me repeat a statement that I made to a group of college students some twenty years ago that is still valid and speaks to the good day and bad day scenarios: *Your worst days are never so bad that you are beyond the* **reach** *of God's grace. And your best days are never so good that you are beyond the* **need** *of God's grace.*

Every day of our lives should be a day of relating to God on the basis of his grace alone, for every day of our lives we are not yet perfect. Someday we will be. Someday each of us will go to be with the Lord (if he does not return first), and at that time we will join the spirits of "the righteous made perfect" (Hebrews 12:23). We look forward to that day with anticipation and hope. In the meantime, despite having died to the dominion of sin through our union with Christ, we still struggle with the presence and activity of sin that remains in us.

So if we are going to grow in the realization of who we are in Christ, we must come to terms with the reality that we are not yet perfect; the presence and activity of sin is still alive and well within us. The reason we must accept this fact is that we cannot look to Christ for our identity if we are still trying to find something about ourselves to prop up our self-esteem. To really grow in the wonderful reality of who we are in Christ, we must abandon any desire to find something within ourselves that makes us acceptable to God.

This does not mean that we should not aspire to grow in holiness, nor does it mean we will never see progress in our lives. It certainly does not mean that we should shrug off the expressions of remaining sin with the thought, "Oh well, that's just the way I am." No, all the moral imperatives in the New Testament imply that we are to seriously pursue growth in Christian character. Consider just a few:

- We are to put off the old self and put on the new self (Ephesians 4:22-24).
- We are to put to death the deeds of the body (Romans 8:13).
- We are to put on such character traits as compassion, kindness, humility, meekness, patience, and love (Colossians 3:12-14).
- We are to abstain from the passions of the flesh, which wage war against our souls (1 Peter 2:11).

- We are to make every effort to grow in all the traits
  of Christian character (2 Peter 1:5-7).

These are just representative of many moral imperatives scattered throughout the New Testament. There is
no question that it is God's will that we pursue a holy and
Christlike life.

But though we are to vigorously pursue spiritual
maturity, both in putting to death sinful traits and putting
on Christlike traits, we must never think that God's
approval and acceptance of us is earned by our progress.
God is obviously *pleased* when we seek to please him
(Colossians 1:10), but his *acceptance* of us is based entirely
on the work of Christ alone in his sinless life and sin-
bearing death.

Let's return to that thought that God is pleased when
we seek to please him. How do our efforts please God? It
is by our motive more than it is our actions. If our motive,
even unconsciously, is to earn God's approval and blessing
by our obedience, then he is not pleased, because that
motive actually demeans the perfect obedience of Christ
in our place. It suggests that the work of Christ on our
behalf was insufficient, so we need to step in and help out.
The motive that God finds acceptable is joyful gratitude
for the fact that Christ has already perfectly obeyed *for us*.

In the previous chapter, I said the concept of Christ's
ownership of our lives is radical and comprehensive. At
the risk of overusing the word *radical*, I want to say that
the motive of obeying God out of gratitude, instead of out
of the assumption that obedience earns God's blessing,

is a radical concept. It is radical in the sense that the vast majority of believers do not understand what it means to be "in Christ" and to find their basic identity in him. They do not understand the truth of our representative union with him so that his obedience becomes our obedience, and his death for sin becomes our death for sin.

Conclusion

My aim in this book has been to help us understand our basic identity. Our answer to the question "Who am I?" is to be found in neither our achievements, nor our failures, nor the evaluations of others, but in Christ alone. It is he who, as our representative before God, lived the perfect life we could never live, died the death we deserved to die, and now sits at the right hand of God, interceding for us— and I suspect, cheering us on.

One of the old Puritans once said, "For every look you take at your sanctification, take two looks at your justification." I want to borrow that sentence structure and say, "For every look you take at yourself in your daily experience, take two looks at who you are in Christ."

May God help all of us to do that.

In this life I am and always will be imperfect, a saved sinner, seeking to grow in holiness and relating to God on the basis of grace that is mie because I am...in Christ!

Dating with Discernment: 12 Questions to Make a Lasting Marriage

Sam A. Andreades / 280 pages

bit.ly/DatingWell

12 QUESTIONS TO MAKE

A LASTING MARRIAGE

DATING
WITH
DISCERNMENT

SAM A.
ANDREADES

"This is a brilliant book!"
Rosaria Butterfield

"This is a brilliant book!" - Rosaria Butterfield
"Provocative and profoundly insightful advice" - Joel Beeke

THE
TEN
COMMANDMENTS
OF
PROGRESSIVE
CHRISTIANITY

MICHAEL J. KRUGER

55 pages / bit.ly/TENCOM

Endorsed by
Collin Hansen, Kevin DeYoung, Michael Horton

DO
MORE
BETTER

A PRACTICAL
GUIDE TO
PRODUCTIVITY

TIM CHALLIES

120 pages

The how and the distinctively Christian why of productivity.

Don't try to do it all.
DO MORE GOOD. BETTER.

www.bit.ly/domorebetter

www.bit.ly/Knowable

Two titles from Peter Krol of DiscipleMakers.

Knowable Word:
Helping Ordinary People Learn to Study the Bible (second edition)

Sowable Word:
Helping Ordinary People Learn to Lead Bible Studies

Endorsements:

Tim Chester
Jerry Bridges
Vern Poythress
Leland Ryken
Ted Tripp
Tim Lane
David Helm
Steve Shadrach
Colleen McFadden
Vince Burens
Jim Elliff
and more

www.bit.ly/Sowable

*Don't miss these fully inductive Bible studies for women
from Keri Folmar!*

Loved by churches. Endorsed by Kristi Anyabwile, Connie Dever,
Gloria Furman, Kathleen Nielson, and Diane Schreiner.

The series currently consists of six volumes.

10 weeks   *10 weeks*   *10 weeks*

Joy! (Philippians)   *Faith* (James)   *Grace* (Ephesians)

11 weeks   *11 weeks*   *9 weeks*

Son of God (Gospel of Mark, 2 volumes)   *Zeal* (Titus)

www.bit.ly/DITWstudies

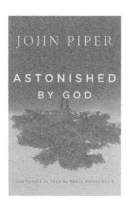

Astonished by God
Ten Truths to Turn the World Upside Down

John Piper | 192 pages

Turn your world on its head.

bit.ly/AstonishedbyGod

Galatians: Redeeming Grace and the Cross of Christ

Melissa McPhail and Lisa Menchinger
184 pages

Introducing the Sophron Series, a new Bible study series for women. Keri Folmar, Series Editor.

bit.ly/Sophron-Galatians

The Joy Project:
An Introduction to Calvinism

(with Study Guide)

Tony Reinke
Foreword by John Piper | 168 pages

True happiness isn't found. It finds you.

bit.ly/JOYPROJECT

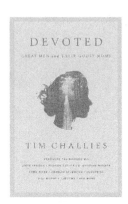

Devoted
Great Men and Their Godly Moms

Tim Challies | 128 pages

Women shaped the men who changed the world.

bit.ly/devotedbook

Run to Win:
The Lifelong Pursuits of a Godly Man

Tim Challies | 163 pages

Plan to run, train to run…run to win.

bit.ly/RUN2WIN

Preparing for Marriage
Help for Christian Couples

John Piper | 86 pages

As you prepare for marriage, dare to dream with God.

bit.ly/prep-for-marriage

"But God..."
The Two Words at the Heart of the Gospel

Casey Lute | 100 pages

Just two words... Understand their use in Scripture, and you will never be the same.

bit.ly/ButGOD

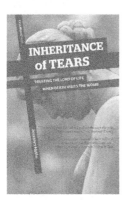

Inheritance of Tears
Trusting the Lord of Life When Death Visits the Womb

Jesssalyn Hutto | 95 pages

Miscarriage: deeply traumatic, tragically common, too often misunderstood.

bit.ly/OFTEARS

The Company We Keep
In Search of Biblical Friendship

Jonathan Holmes
Foreword by Ed Welch | 112 pages

Biblical friendship is deep, honest, pure, tranparent, and liberating. It is also attainable.

bit.ly/B-Friend

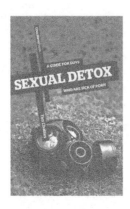

Sexual Detox
A Guide for Guys Who Are Sick of Porn

Tim Challies | 90 pages

Reorient your understanding of sex, according to God's plan for this great gift.

bit.ly/SEXUALDETOX

Intentional Parenting
Family Discipleship by Design

Tad Thompson | 99 pages

The Big Picture and a simple plan—that's what you need to do family discipleship well

bit.ly/IParent

Grieving, Hope and Solace
When a Loved One Dies in Christ

Albert N. Martin | 112 pages

There is comfort for the grief. There are answers to the questions.

bit.ly/GriefHope

Made in the USA
Monee, IL
12 September 2022

13825682R00059